vernon watkins

unity of the stream

vernon watkins

unity of the stream

SELECTED POEMS

BLACK SWAN BOOKS

Published by

BLACK SWAN BOOKS Ltd.
P. O. Box 327
Redding Ridge, CT 06876

ISBN 0-933806-05-1

CONTENTS

unity
of the
stream

FOREWORD

I am grateful to the Academi Gymreig for the opportunity to present this selection of Vernon Watkins's poetry. It contains poems from Ballad of the Mari Lwyd, The Lady with the Unicorn, The Death Bell, Cypress and Acacia, Affinities, Fidelities and Uncollected Poems, all now out of print. The earliest poems date from the thirties and the latest from just before his death in 1967; and it is characteristic of his poetry that over a span of thirty years it remains true to the same centre and concerned with the same themes. All Vernon Watkins's poetry is pre-occupied, as Roland Mathias has pointed out, with the conquest of time. Whatever the explicit theme, the underlying one is always the poet's exaltation of the permanence of art and "the Christian paradox" against the transience of grief and the passing years. Because of this, any selection of his poems will have an inherent unity.

Vernon Watkins chose the poems for all his books after a pattern in his own mind. I have made this selection in the same way. The "pattern" is that of a river, which rises in spring, childhood, and the first freshness of the poetic impulse, running on through many landscapes to autumn, old age and death. The poems are grouped according to theme, but the themes should not be regarded separately; each poem, and each theme, should throw light on the following one. All the Music of Colours poems are here printed together for the first time, as are all the Taliesin poems.

My thanks are due to Roland Mathias for sharing the task of selecting the poems; and to Ruth Pryor and Tristan Watkins for advice and assistance on dating, on the notes, and in preparing the typescript.

The date at the end of each poem is that of first publication. Readers interested in the chronology of the various themes should, however, remember that the interval of time between the first draft of a poem and its first publication may vary from a few weeks to twenty-five years.

Pennard Cliffs   GWEN WATKINS
January 1978

Unity of the Stream

Take this into account:
Like water from a fount
Until it reach the sea,
Song is unique delight;
You cannot snap its flight
Like wood across your knee.

You cannot tear apart
The single jet of art
That glitters there entire.
The innocent is bound
To wisdom in the ground
Of that revealing fire.

Song is all mastery
And first virginity;
Without it time were vain.
It lives to make love fly
Through nuptials of the sky
And feed the earth like rain.

1963

Poets, in Whom Truth Lives

Poets, in whom truth lives
Until you say you know,
Gone are the birds; the leaves
Drop, drift away, and snow
Surrounds you where you sing,
A silent ring.

Lives of the dead you share,
Earth-hid, in tender trust.
Passion builds the air;
The beautiful and just
Through your tongues' ecstasy
Can hear and see.

Christ, where the cold stream ran
Which now lies locked in doubt,
A proud cock-pheasant can
Stretching its plumage out
More praise you than the rest
With his gold crest.

So hear those shepherds come,
Drawn by a secret fire,
Though Vergil's voice is dumb
Proclaiming to the lyre,
Through time by Winter torn,
The boy, new-born.

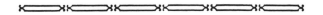

The abounding river stops.
Time in a flash grows less
True than these glittering drops
Caught on a thread of glass
Two frosty branches bear
In trance-like air.

Stoop; for the hollow ground
Integrity yet keeps
True as a viol's sound
Though the musician sleeps.
Strong is your trust; then wait:
Your King comes late.

1951

Touch with Your Fingers

Touch with your fingers
The strings of song.
Love runs deeper
Than all time's wrong.
I have considered
Such things long.

Banishing waters
Bore it once.
D'Orléans looked
Towards the coast of France.
Florence exiled
Her noblest sons.

Under the rising
Spectral moon
Rome, Alexandria,
Babylon,
Athens and Carthage
Rise in stone.

Time that is over
Comes not again;
Yet instinctive
The strings remain.
All is fugitive,
Nothing vain.

Magical foliage
Glittering shone.
There they trembled
Who now are gone.
Dancers perish:
The dance goes on.

What then compelled me
To take on trust
Words of the poets
Laid in dust?
Time cannot answer.
True love must.

Love is compounded
Of all it cast.
Sacred forgiveness
Binds all fast.
Timeless vision
Discerns no Past.

Shade of Calliope,
Guard my days.
Such compassion
From dust I raise,
Nothing is valid
Except that praise.

1956

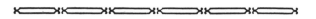

Swallows over the Weser

Dark in their dipping and rising the swallows fly over the
Weser.
Here in the buttercups lying, we watch them, nor long to be
wiser
Than day; but to fly like the swallows, to dip and to rise,
were a deftness,
A daring, a language of movement, a gracefulness,
something surpassing
Ecstasy. Keen the wild swallow can see the quick waters
beneath her.
We through the buttercup-grasses can see the black star of
her shadow
Scintillate now on the water and cut like a scythe through
the grasses
Green in the sun. Here to lie, here to dream on the
Summersoft meadow
Watching their wings in the sunlight, their wings that
transfix the bright aether,
Diamondly flying, is lovely. Low diving, they skim where
the branches
Of sycamore darken the river, jade leaves in a thunder-light
glassing
With terror the marble-dark mover, caught up where the
sun-dazzle blanches
Their underside shot on a wheel, revolution revealing each
feather,
Then gone: O the dark and the fair one, the gloom and the
glory, not either
Still for a moment! But we, lying back, see the flash and the
damask
Blue sash of their darting, their distance, then fragile, the
far-away fleeces

And movement of wind-gathered clouds; so we watch
　　them through goldcups that wither
Fly over the ferns of the weir, where the water like
　　quicksilver ceases
Or burns in a dragonfly sailing, now lost in the light of the
　　morning,
Touching with fingers this doom of the close thing
　　eternally passing.

1947

Crowds

Why should the living need my oil?
I see them, and their eyes are blest.
No. For those others I must toil:
I toil to set the dead at rest.

Yet when I watch in solemn tides
The drifting crowds, each life a ghost,
I mourn them, for their truth abides;
Nor is one loved, till he is lost.

1943

Fidelity to the Dead

The withered leaf is blest, and the bird with shrunk claw
    in the shingle.
Under the shawl the life-yielding hand has caught the
    passionate thread.
Immortal silence transfigures them. O ultimate faith found
    single,
O light of intense meditation, from you the timid have fled.

Love steals from the fortunate man and gives to the heart it
    bereaves.
Dark thunders descend on Prometheus. A light over Earth
    is shed.
How, with love's great example, could I fear what the blind
    Fate weaves?
Love is fidelity to the unfortunate dead.

                                1945

Fidelity to the Living

Tenuous life, I have wronged you. You are the leaves, the
  sun,
The light, the bird at peace in the sky, though pulled by a
  plummet of lead.
Out of dark books I accused you. O look at her face: there is
  spun
A thread of light from her silence: she holds that beautiful
  thread.

The mother lifts the child to her breast. O what infinite,
  tender
Frailty! She laughs near his eyelids: O, above Solomon
  blest!
The great magnanimous leaves have opened. Plucked from
  their judgment in splendour,
Even now, by the very thread which binds them, they are at
  rest.

1945

Ballad of the Trial of Sodom

God came to Abram,
Abram the man
Who knew no glory
Could resist God's ban,
And God said: *"Abram,*
I come to destroy
Sodom, Sodom,
Sodom, Sodom,
That golden city
Of sin and joy."

Thunder. Thunder. Thunder. Thunder.
Death is terrible, a thing of wonder.
First is a lethargy that no man likes,
Then comes the moment when the lightning
      strikes.

Then Abram, trying
To save that place,
Thinking of the dying,
Fell upon his face.
"Lord, if there were fifty
Righteous men
In Sodom, Sodom,
Sodom, Sodom,
Men who were steadfast,
Would you destroy it then?"

Heaven knows what payment
An advocate should ask,
But old man Abram
Had the hardest task.

He looked at Sodom
And he heard God's voice:
"Sodom, Sodom,
Sodom, Sodom;
Hide not the city
That my hand destroys."

And Abram was trying
To save that place.
He lay for a long time
And could not lift his face.
"White though the lightning
Where the thunder rolls
Towards Sodom, Sodom,
Sodom, Sodom,
I shall not destroy it
If there are fifty souls."

And Abram pondered.
He could not make amends.
It lightened and thundered.
He counted up his friends.
"Lord God, have patience.
May flesh be left alive
In Sodom, Sodom,
Sodom, Sodom,
That doomed city,
If the fifty lack five?"

The Lord God darkened
Like a fiery cloud.
Abram waited
As he lay there bowed;
He saw Hell's demons
In a midnight dive
In Sodom, Sodom,
Sodom, Sodom.
*"I shall not destroy it
For the forty-and-five."*

"Lord God, have patience.
Destruction is just;
To hide the accursed
In the darkest dust.
But should there be forty
In the temple found
Of Sodom, Sodom,
Sodom, Sodom,
Then would you brand it,
Raze it to the ground?"

Abram breathed.
A long breath he took.
He thought of the temple,
And the temple shook.
Monsters of sacrilege
Sprawled where it stood
In Sodom, Sodom,
Sodom, Sodom.
*"I would not brand it
For the forty good."*

And Abram knew,
Abram knew,
This was the hardest
Peace for which to sue.
"Lord God, forgive me
That I should speak again
Of Sodom, Sodom,
Sodom, Sodom.
Would you spare the city
For thirty good men?"

Thunder. Thunder. Thunder. Thunder.
Death is terrible, a thing of wonder.
First is a lethargy that no man likes,
Then comes the moment when the lightning
    strikes.

And Abram counted.
Try as he would,
He could not make the number up
To thirty good.
The Judgment's answer
Came upon him then:
"Tell Sodom, Sodom,
Sodom, Sodom,
I shall not destroy it
For thirty good men."

Abram was silent.
Abram was dumb.
He heard Hell's demons
Beating on a drum.
He saw men carried
Under long, slim poles
Through Sodom, Sodom,
Sodom, Sodom.
"Lord, would you save it
For twenty souls?"

This was the last time.
This was the last.
Now for the brimstone
And the blinding blast.
He saw huge darkness
Like a hangman's hood
On Sodom, Sodom,
Sodom, Sodom.
*"I still would spare it
For the twenty good."*

"Lord, Thou art just.
Lord, Thou art just.
How should we utter
Who are less than dust?

Yet so wicked
Are the hearts of men
In Sodom, Sodom,
Sodom, Sodom.
Still would you spare it
If the good were ten?"

Fearful the silence,
Fearful the span
Stretching that moment
Between God and man.
Abram sweated
His life out then
For Sodom, Sodom,
Sodom, Sodom.
"I shall not destroy it
If the good are ten."

Abram the father
Counting up the cost
Saw faith plainly
And knew that he had lost.
God looked at Sodom
In that pleading place,
Sodom, Sodom,
Sodom, Sodom.
Down looked Abram,
And he lost his case.

1953

Ballad of Culver's Hole

What feet are heard about these rocks
This highest tide of the year?
White spray of the equinox,
You chill the heart with fear.

Two boats close in from East and West
On a little boat that feels
The lucky weight of Culver
Gripping the stolen creels.

Is it the rope of Culver
Where the shag has the wit to dive,
Dragged through the shivering breakers,
That makes these rocks alive?

A great, round barrel
He has rolled up that grey beach.
Voices like claws are closing in,
Almost within reach.

In a moment he has vanished.
The gully's packed with dread.
Where is he hiding in the rocks,
The man they took for dead?

"Between this headland and that point
He surely ran aground.
Who saw the cunning hare stop dead
To cheat the flying hound?

You up there, on the cliff's dark brows,
You who stand there stiff,
Where does Culver keep his house,
Perched upon what cliff?"

"We know nothing, we know nothing,
Never found his nest.
Ours is the crooked haystack,
The white-washed farm at rest.

We hear nothing, we hear nothing,
Only seabirds' cries.
Call his name to the rock, and then
Hear what the rock replies.

A white-washed cottage, a house of stone
Might not hold your man.
Out of a nest of bleaching bone
The brightest fisher sprang.

We have seen the kestrel hang in the air
And where the ravens glide
Have combed the rocks for laver-bread
And the cockles in the tide.

But danger haunts the upper ledge
Here where the seagull flies.
Why do you ask us gently
With murder in your eyes?

Watch, watch your footing.
The stones in the ledge are loose.
Under this hollow cliff the sea
Is hissing like a goose."

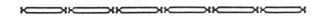

"Let two upon the green turf go
And two upon the rocks.
A great tide is running,
On the door of death it knocks.

It roars to have him hammered down
With nails to the sea bed.
Where is he hiding in the rocks,
The man we took for dead?"

"The equinox is rising;
The sky to the West is black.
The sea has drowned a hundred pools:
Should we not go back?"

"To think, that fish was in my net
And now has got away.
He beckons for the sun to set
And the waters fill the bay."

"Go back, go back, and leave him
Before it is too late.
The sea has drowned a thousand pools.
We cannot fight with Fate.

The great rock and the little rock,
They slip beneath the wave.
These breakers have drawn blood before,
Their lilies strewn a grave.

The mole beneath the giant sea
Is heaping mound on mound.
Make for the ship, come quickly,
Or we shall all be drowned."

"The dark is helping the digging mole
To cut our exit off.
Who could smoke out a smuggler's hole
In a sea so blind and rough?

God rot the guts of Culver
By whom the good man dies.
He laughs behind a wall of rock
Where every rock has eyes."

Now each rock wears disguises,
Each darkened stone deceives,
And louder the wave rises
With a noise of rustling leaves.

But before the long wave hit the ground
The shag had the wit to dive.
Those greyhounds covered at a bound
The hare they left alive.

Their noose is for that goose of the sea,
But they have not caught him yet.
A barrel rises slowly
Just where the sun had set.

1952

Rhossili

Pushed out from the rocks, pushed far by old thought, long
   into night, under starlight,
At last, tired from my coastal labouring, I come to you,
   sleepless Rhossili.
I have cut through the mirror-bright sea in the long, slender
   boat with two paddles,
And ground in the sand. Dawn breaks. I stare, amazed, at
   the marvel.

Coiled sand, gold mountains, grass-tufted dunes, unending,
   rising, descending,
And the cat-spotted, wind-crafty tide, spitting serpent-
   white tongues drawn slack,
Soon reaching the barnacled wreck, quivering, recoiling,
   bending
Stung eyes to the rasping whisper of gongs, of songs that
   will not run back.

Rhossili! Spindle of the moon! Turning-place of winds, end
   of Earth, and of Gower!
Last one, shivering like a shell, cold with thought that is
   fiery and new!
A tent-pole. The cries of seabirds. And over our fingers the
   power
Of perplexing starlight, entangling our threads in the field
   soaked with dew.

Worm's Head! The rock of Tiresias' eyes! From the world's
   very verge
I listen to the locked bell-ringers, the impetuous thunder
   and crash
Of the flying, flagellant waves, torn into two by the surge

From the strata of winkle-stuck rocks, and caverns where
claw-mussels flash.

Terrified, the nesting-birds mount as I climb. Mantles of
fugitive blue
Drain blood, and the bull of the sea falls pierced in the
spindrift dance.
Up from the mirror of the waters to the summit a seabird
flew.
I creep to the verge of the pard-breathing tide. Cries turn
round the rock's turning lance.

Flat on my face I lie, near the needle around which the
wide world spins.
Three eggs are balanced there, mottled in cushion-soft,
quicksilver grass, on the final rock.
Far out in the deep blue water the razorbills fish, and their
skins
Dazzle, where they flutter blown wings drenched white,
nor scatter, nor break their flock.

I watch them like bright-winged ants, on the deep,
unresting swell
Where they rise and fall, fly clear of the crest, or hover
with sea-touching wings.
High overhead wheel the herring-gulls, each with a
plummet; they drop, and a bell
Rocks in each bird, swung away by a thread, spun out from
these rock-rooted things.

Sheer down they rush at my head, crazy with fear for the
loss
Of their locked, unawakened young, hidden in those brown
shells

On a perilous ledge. They scream; and their wings divide
and cross
In a shuddering shadow of piston-like bones, in a rain of
farewells.

From the navel of rock, birth's pinnacle, the hovering wings
hurled wide,
Flying out and ever returning to this unseen point of fear,
Watch witchcraft, the snakelike movement of the
enchanted tide.
I reach to the razorbills' verge. My fingers clutch the rock
spear.

Light screams: Look down at the mad, mazed frenzy of the
destroying moon!
Gasp at the cockle-sucked heaven! Tide-blown the
castaways lie
Peeled to the parched and weary grains where the beaked
ships spin and are gone.
Blood-light on the wings of the sea! O the bull and the
dragonfly!

The Sibyl keeps watch for Tiresias. In the dumb yet singing
rock
The brother of light is dead, or sleeping, transfixed like a
shell in a cleft,
In a thunder of floundering timbers, where pine-logs and
rum-barrels knock.
Sun-dazzled the book-leaves have opened; but only his
vision is left.

Look! The sea-threads! Thought begins there! In a million
    rainbows! The zenith
Stares at the long flat beach, no bend, no break in the dance
Of sandgrains and seawaves, drenched in gold spray, where
    the downs fly on to Llangennith:
Dolphins, plunging from death into birth, you are held by
    the Sibyl's trance!

1943

Taliesin in Gower

Late I return, O violent, colossal, reverberant,
  eavesdropping sea.
My country is here. I am foal and violet. Hawthorn breaks
  from my hands.
I watch the inquisitive cormorant pry from the praying
  rock of Pwlldu,
Then skim to the gulls' white colony, to Oxwich's
  cocklestrewn sands.

I have seen the curlew's triangular print, I know every inch
  of his way.
I have gone through the door of the foundered ship, I have
  slept in the winch of the cave
With pine-log and unicorn-spiral shell secreting the
  colours of day;
I have been taught the script of the stones, and I know the
  tongue of the wave.

I witness here in a vision the landscape to which I was
  born,
Three smouldering bushes of willow, like trees of fire, and
  the course
Of the river under the stones of death, carrying the ear of
  corn
Withdrawn from the moon-dead chaos of rocks
  overlooking its secret force.

I see, a marvel in Winter's marshes, the iris break from its
  sheath
And the dripping branch in the ache of sunrise frost and
  shadow redeem

With wonder of patient, living leaf, while Winter, season of
    death,
Rebukes the sun, and grinds out men's groans in the voice
    of its underground stream.

Yet now my task is to weigh the rocks on the level wings of
    a bird,
To relate these undulations of time to a kestrel's motionless
    poise.
I speak, and the soft-running hour-glass answers; the core
    of the rock is a third:
Landscape survives, and these holy creatures proclaim
    their regenerate joys.

I know this mighty theatre, my footsole knows it for mine.
I am nearer the rising pewit's call than the shiver of her
    own wing.
I ascend in the loud waves' thunder, I am under the last of
    the nine.
In a hundred dramatic shapes I perish, in the last I live and
    sing.

All that I see with my sea-changed eyes is a vision too great
    for the brain.
The luminous country of auk and eagle rocks and shivers
    to earth.
In the hunter's quarry this landscape died; my vision
    restores it again.
These stones are prayers; every boulder is hung on a
    breath's miraculous birth.

Gorse breaks on the steep cliff-side, clings earth, in patches
    blackened for sheep,
For grazing fired; now the fair weather comes to the ravens'
    pinnacled knoll.
Larks break heaven from the thyme-breathing turf; far
    under, flying through sleep,
Their black fins cutting the rainbow surf, the porpoises
    follow the shoal.

They are gone where the river runs out, there where the
    breakers divide
The lacework of Three Cliffs Bay in a music of two seas
A heron flaps where the sandbank holds a dyke to the
    twofold tide,
A wave-encircled isthmus of sound which the white bird-
    parliament flees.

Rhinoceros, bear and reindeer haunt the crawling glaciers
    of age
Beheld in the eye of the rock, where a javelin'd arm held
    stiff,
Withdrawn from the vision of flying colours, reveals, like
    script on a page,
The unpassing moment's arrested glory, a life locked fast in
    the cliff.

Now let the great rock turn. I am safe with an ear of corn,
A repository of light once plucked, from all men hidden
    away.
I have passed through a million changes. In a butterfly
    coracle borne,
My faith surmounting the Titan, I greet the prodigious bay.

I celebrate you, marvellous forms. But first I must cut the
    wood,
Exactly measure the strings, to make manifest what shall
    be.
All Earth being weighed by an ear of corn, all heaven by a
    drop of blood.
How shall I loosen this music to the listening,
    eavesdropping sea?

1950

Taliesin and the Spring of Vision

"I tread the sand at the sea's edge, sand of the hour-glass,
And the sand receives my footprint, singing:
'You are my nearmost, you who have travelled the farthest,
And you are my constant, who have endured all
    vicissitudes
In the cradle of sea, Fate's hands, and the spinning waters.
The measure of past grief is the measure of present joy.
Your tears, which have dried to Chance, now spring from a
    secret.
Here time's glass breaks, and the world is transfigured in
    music.' "

So sang the grains of sand, and while they whirled to a
    pattern
Taliesin took refuge under the unfledged rock.
He could not see in the cave, but groped with his hand,
And the rock he touched was the socket of all men's eyes,
And he touched the spring of vision. He had the mind of a
    fish
That moment. He knew the glitter of scale and fin.
He touched the pin of pivotal space, and he saw
One sandgrain balance the ages' cumulus cloud.

Earth's shadow hung. Taliesin said: "The penumbra of
    history is terrible.
Life changes, breaks, scatters. There is no sheet-anchor.
Time reigns; yet the kingdom of love is every moment,
Whose citizens do not age in each other's eyes.
In a time of darkness the pattern of life is restored
By men who make all transience seem an illusion
Through inward acts, acts corresponding to music.
Their works of love leave words that do not end in the
    heart."

He still held rock. Then three drops fell on his fingers,
And Future and Past converged in a lightning flash:
"It was we who instructed Shakespeare, who fell upon
      Dante's eyes,
Who opened to Blake the Minute Particulars. We are the
      soul's rebirth."

Taliesin answered: "I have encountered the irreducible
      diamond
In the rock. Yet now it is over. Omniscience is not for man.
Christen me, therefore, that my acts in the dark may be
      just,
And adapt my partial vision to the limitation of time."

1952

Taliesin's Voyage

The coracle carried me.
The seawave tossed me.
Hawk, hound harried me.
Caridwen lost me.

Hid in the hollow
Of a rounded bark,
I heard swift, swallow,
Fly through the dark.

Raved, nor remembered
Earthly things,
But wide-ribbed, slumbered
Under those wings.

Past day and night,
Past night and day,
Under the flight
Of the stars I lay.

At last emerging
With dawn I woke
Where rough seas surging
On shingle broke.

Caridwen's prey,
Child of the sea,
I was cast that day
On wild Pwlldu.

The days of my voyage
When numbered are
As a glacier's age
Or a shooting star.

Swift and slow
In one rope twined,
A sail did throw
On my dreaming mind.

Time I pursued
And saw the kill.
Life was renewed
Where time lay still.

Sand and the year
That seemed deranged
Are filled with grandeur,
For all is changed.

O raven, kestrel,
Wheeling round,
Teach your minstrel
The heart of sound!

I, Taliesin,
Know the cords
Between that pin
And the turning birds.

But the wind's hound
And the mussel's sting
Between the drowned
And the seabird's wing,

Where have they left
Destruction's key,
Hid in what cleft
Of the crying sea?

1953

Taliesin and the Mockers

Before men walked
I was in these places.
I was here
When the mountains were laid.

I am as light
To eyes long blind,
I, the stone
Upon every grave.

I saw black night
Flung wide like a curtain.
I looked up
At the making of stars.

I stood erect
At the birth of rivers.
I observed
The designing of flowers.

Who has discerned
The voice of lightning,
Or traced the music
Behind the eyes?

My Lord prescribed
The paths of the planets.
His fingers scattered
The distant stars.

He shaped the grave shore's
Ringing stones
And gave to the rocks
An echoing core.

He bound great mountains
With snow and ice
And bathed in glory
The lesser hills.

He made the sun
Of sulphurous fire.
From secret darkness
He called the moon.

Under her voice
And moving light
He chained the tides
Of the great seas rolling.

Still upon Earth
Was no live creature.
Barren still
Was the womb of the sea.

Mute the features
Slept in the rock,
Limbs and the soul
Inert, unbeckoned.

Marrowed with air
He made the birds.
Fish He sowed
In the restless wave.

Antelope, horse
And bull He made.
From caves of ice
He released the stormwinds.

He numbered the meadow's
Drops of rain
Caught in the cloud
And the teeming rose-bush.

Lions He made
Like fallen suns,
Fiery sand
And the beasts of burden.

He gave to the trees
Mysterious fruits
And twined in the husk
Miraculous corn.

Where lizards breathed
On the pathless desert
He gave each atom
A hidden sun.

Last, all labour
He bent on dust.
Out of the red dust
Made He Man.

Ancient music
Of silence born:
All things born
At the touch of God.

He built for him
His eternal garden,
Timeless, moving,
And yet in time.

He cast on him
Dark veils of sleep.
Out of his side
He took the Female.

Ask my age:
You shall have no answer.
I saw the building
Of Babel's Tower.

I was a lamp
In Solomon's temple;
I, the reed
Of an auguring wind.

What do you seek
In the salmon river,
Caught in the net,
What living gold?

What do you seek
In the weir, O Elphin?
You must know
That the sun is mine.

I have a gift
For I have nothing.
I have love
Which excels all treasures.

Certain there were
Who touched, who knew Him.
Blind men knew
On the road their God.

Mock me they will,
Those hired musicians,
They at Court
Who command the schools.

Mock though they do,
My music stands
Before and after
Accusing silence.

1955

Taliesin at Pwlldu

Through leaning boughs I see the veil of heaven,
Through leaf-ears fluted from ancestral playing
To inward darkness, to the windblown tree,
Marvel of time, caught in a living cell,
Daphne enshrined, in this pure moment given
To air, all leaves!
    I look, and hear them saying:
"In boundless light only the bound are free";
And music flows through me as through a shell.

Clear is the shell upon these watery sands
And, washed with light, leaves break in these dark woods.
Streams dance and glitter, and the rocks have veins.
My Master from the rainbow on the sea
Launched my round bark. Through darkness, trailing
   hands,
I drifted. Wave-gnarled images of gods
Floated upon the whale-backed water-plains.
I looked; creation rose, upheld by Three.

And there are three about me where I stand.
Ah secret place within the source of tears
Caught by stream's light, uniting all that's gone:
Pure stream, by pebbles masked and changing skies,
I touch you; then I know my native land.
Pride cast the pattern from primaeval years,
The avenger's knives in glacier-driven stone
Changed by God's peace, transfixed where morning flies.

Earlier version 1953
Revised 1966

Sea Chant

(Taliesin to Venus)

Venus, Loreley-breasted,
   Ceaseless mother of change,
      Born where the rainbow shivers
         Bright from the breaking wave,
Rocked where the seabird rested,
   Did you not charm the strange
      Boats from the various rivers
         Into a single grave?

Sprung from merciless weathers
   Hard and hostile to man,
      You that have launched and shaken
         Ships, and destroyed so much,
Why should a crest and feathers
   Which in wild air began,
      Wheeling, dive and awaken
         All that you dare not touch?

Patterning sunbeams serve you,
   Doves, and pinks in the rock,
      Drenched where the spray of breakers
         Flies to the ravens' nest.
Who but I can preserve you
   Chaste, from shudder and shock?
      See: all others forsake us;
         Only the dead have rest.

Yet that golden-eyed egret
   Still as a hawk shall stay,
      While you proclaim to islands
         Nothing dark shall endure.

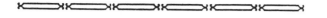

I have discerned a secret
  Hid from the arc of day,
    Locked in the heart of silence,
      Stronger than death, and pure.

Lacework pattern of fingers
  Spun and cast by the wave,
    Brilliance a rainbow scatters,
      Bride-veils falling away:
I, the last of your singers,
  See how the shells you gave
    Shine where the breaker shatters
      All that we know of day.

Just as Semele's wonder
  Looked for the thunder's truth,
    So, as the breakers whitening
      Crash on the brittle shore,
Out of a clap of thunder
  Springs an immortal youth:
    He who is born of lightning
      Lives under time no more.

I, with strength from the giver,
  Kindling coral and horn,
    Taught by the tides of ages,
      Take you, at last subdued.
I am come to deliver
  You, of the white spray born.
    Do not all faiths and sages
      End in a child their feud?

                                      1968

The Tributary Seasons

I can discern at last how grew
This tree, so naked and so true.
"Spring was my death; when all is sung,
It was the Autumn made me young."

Midwinter: packed with ice the butt,
Splitting its sides.
Roots hard as iron; the back door shut.
Heaped wood a ringing axe divides.
Sacks on the pipes. No river flows,
No tap, no spring. A skater goes
Skimming across the pond. A stone
Stays on the ice where it is thrown.
Under a bone a blue-tit swings,
The keen light glancing on his wings.
To robins crusts and crumbs are tossed,
Yellow against the white of frost.
A quilted world. Glazed mistletoe.
Spades glint, and sledges glide, on snow.
Boys scoop it up with tingling hands,
Steadying the snowman where he stands,
Numb into dusk. Then holly boughs
Darken the walls in many a house,
While moth-flakes pile on wood and ground,
Muffling the panes, and hide all sound.
     The tree of Winter, Winter's tree:
     Winter a dark, a naked tree.

What you have seen you have not known.
Look for it now that Winter's gone.
The Winter stars, the silent king,
The angelic night, give way to Spring.

March into May: the lengthening day
With forward light
Kindles the finches in their play,
Turning their wings in amorous flight.
No star in frost more brightly shines
Than, in white grass, these celandines.
Now sunlight warms and light wind shakes
The unopened blooms. The jonquil breaks
Clean from its sheath. Gold wax and gums
Hold the buds fast. The chestnut comes
First into leaf, its trance-bound hands
Pulled from the shell by silken strands,
Breathless and white. The sap unseen
Climbs the stiff stalk and makes all green.
All timeless coils break through, sublime,
The skins and cerements of time.
What spikenard makes the dark earth sweet?
Life from the hyacinth's winding-sheet
Breathes on the fields, and thrushes sing:
"Earth is our mother. Spring is Spring."
    The tree of Spring, the selfsame tree:
    Spring is the green, foretelling tree.

    What you have seen you cannot know.
    Winter is gone, and Spring will go.
    These blossoms falling through long grass
    Will fade from swallows' quivering glass.

Now the meridian. Summer glows,
A furnace weighed,
Deep in red rose and burnet rose,
Entranced by its own musk and shade.
Birds sing more softly. Foxgloves keep
Over the hedge a misty sleep.

Gardens are secret in their walls
And mountains feel their waterfalls.
Murmuring among thick blooms, the bees
Plunge, and in silence honey seize,
Then bear it droning to their hive
Of light by labour kept alive.
Yet still the toil, where leaves are dense,
Breathes of the Spring's first frankincense.
Butterflies dance in blazing beams.
Great trees are hushed, and still the streams.
On river banks, where boughs serene
Reflect their every shade of green,
Bathers take rest, and bodies come
Naked to peace, and their first home.
　　　The tree of Summer, Summer's tree,
　　　Lost in the sleep of Adam's tree.

　　　Might this indeed have been the prime,
　　　That Eden state of lasting time?
　　　Men reap the grain and tend the vine,
　　　Heaping their tributes, bread and wine.

At last late leaves bright-coloured bring,
Turning time's keys,
Those fruits foreshadowed by the Spring.
Acorns and nuts restore their trees.
As certain jewels have the power
To magnetize and guide the hour,
So seeds before our eyes are strewn
Fast hidden in the pod's cocoon.
These die, yet in themselves they keep
All seasons cradled in their sleep.
Guarding the lost through calms and storms,
These are the year's eternal forms,

An alphabet whose letters all
Mark out a sacred festival.
The birth of vision from these urns
Into whose silence dust returns
Fills the dense wood. Saint Hubert' ; rein
Stops the swift horse; for there again
A stag between its antlers holds
Heaven's unique glory, and the world's.
  Tree of beginning, Autumn tree:
  Divine imagination's tree.

1955

Returning to Goleufryn

Returning to my grandfather's house, after this exile
From the coracle-river, long left with a coin to be good,
Returning with husks of those venturing ears for food
To lovely Carmarthen, I touch and remember the turnstile
Of this death-bound river. Fresh grass. Here I find that
        crown
In the shadow of dripping river-wood; then look up to the
        burning mile
Of windows. It is Goleufryn, the house on the hill;
And picking a child's path in a turn of the Towy I meet the
        prodigal town.

Sing, little house, clap hands: shut, like a book of the
        Psalms,
On the leaves and pressed flowers of a journey. All is
        sunny
In the garden behind you. The soil is alive with blind-
        petalled blooms
Plundered by bees. Gooseberries and currants are gay
With tranquil, unsettled light. Breathless light begging alms
Of the breathing grasses bent over the river of tombs
Flashes. A salmon has swallowed the tribute-money
Of the path. On the farther bank I see ragged urchins play

With thread and pin. O lead me that I may drown
In those earlier cobbles, reflected; a street that is strewn
        with palms,
Rustling with blouses and velvet. Yet I alone
By the light in the sunflower deepening, here stand, my
        eyes cast down
To the footprint of accusations, and hear the faint,
        leavening

Music of first Welsh words; that gust of plumes
"They shall mount up like eagles," dark-throated assumes,
Cold-sunned, low thunder and gentleness of the authentic
    Throne.

Yet now I am lost, lost in the water-wound looms
Where brief, square windows break on a garden's decay.
Gold butter is shining, the tablecloth speckled with crumbs.
The kettle throbs. In the calendar harvest is shown,
Standing in sheaves. Which way would I do you wrong?
Low, crumbling doorway of the infirm to the mansions of
    evening,
And poor, shrunken furrow where the potatoes are sown,
I shall not unnumber one soul I have stood with and known
To regain your stars struck by horses, your sons of God
    breaking in song.

1943

Llewelyn's Chariot

Sun of all suns, seed of dandelion seeds,
Sprung from the stem of delight and the starry course,
High at the helm of night, in the van of deeds,
A one-wheeled carriage you drive and a headless horse.
Your Maker makes you his glory, you grasp and push
Through bars the bugle, the mirror, the string of beads,
The doll and the wooden men; with a mighty wish
You ride the brunt of creation's galloping beds.

What golden fleece enshrines at the very prow
Your marvelling head, and summons from ancient seas
Sailors toiling, under the black sea-crow,
What ever-moving, miraculous, wind-faint fleece;
But you kick those puppets, those men of deeds, through
    the bars,
The tossed men lost, the lost men under the ark,
Seed of spray's seed, swept from the flight of the stars
To a point of light in your look that is almost dark.

Rameses, trumpet and chariot, all you outrun
Grasping your cage where grief is banished for good,
Created nothing, timeless, perpetual one
Dropped from light-years to crawl under legs of wood,
Star-seed, breath-downed, dropped from the topmost sun
To the toppling house near the shed that shadows a hearse
From whirling, luminous night, to sleep here alone
In the darkness a great light leaves, where a feather stirs.

And I, your listener, stopped on the stairway of breath,
Awake, in the stranger's bed, in the cold, high room,
Calling the sea from Leviathan hollows of earth,
I watch them, castaway toys, while you drive and boom

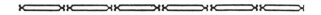

Your course in the cot to my bed, with the speed of ice,
The giant mirror, the trumpet ringed with a bell,
Till naked you stand, gold-fleeced, shaping a shell,
All seas to your colour, Llewelyn, child above price.

1943

The Caryatids
(for Rhiannon asleep)

How still the Caryatids
Hold up their sleeping urns
Above the dreaming lids
Hark, and the wash returns
Of time's remembered wrack.
Loud the wave breaks, and loud
The dragging wash ebbs back,
Threading a moonlit shroud.

In dread of lightning now
A towering breaker brings
Blackness beneath the Plough
And scatters seabirds' wings
Sleeping upon its crest.
The wild Earth wanders there
Stunned by the moon's unrest
Where seaweeds like gold hair

Cling to a dazzling shell.
Cold are these waters, cold
The tales no lips can spell
Asleep in that white fold;
Yet the grave arms how strong,
Supporting, while seas broke,
The balanced urns of song,
Under the lightning-stroke.

Aggressive candour plays
Already in your eyes
Teaching you daring ways,
Lending your bold replies

An elemental charm
Pure as the light of dawn.
And how could I disarm
A truth so finely drawn

From the dark sheath of sleep?
You are not six years old;
Yet the first wash will keep,
Whatever life re-mould
With brush or palette-knife
Afterwards on the page.
And I, who watch your life
Against the uncertain age

Momentously at rest,
Already see divined
The joy by which we are blest
Moving in eyes declined.
How should I pray? My prayer
Found in closed eyelids stands
While seawaves pierce night's air
And pound the unyielding sands.

There all the reckoned grains
Obey the rock-like Word
Whose lightning love remains,
Waiting to be restored.
And still how patiently
They watch above your bed,
Nor touch the form I see.
Like footprints on the sea,
How near is love to dread!

1951

The Precision of the Wheel
(to my son)

How like a wheel of prayer
The year returns,
Precision plucked from air;
And the soul learns
The rustling of those trees,
The changing sound,
Music of cypresses
In hallowed ground
And of that younger green
Which drops its blooms
Sudden as swallows, seen
When April comes.

Your birthday; and, that night,
I stopped, to bind
What I had come to write.
That month my mind
Had run upon a coil
Where light newborn
Revealed in weaver's toil
Lady and unicorn.
The sixfold tapestry
In my mind's eye
Held darkness searchingly;
And then your cry.

Twelve years since then have passed,
And to the day
This verse arrives, my last;
And I must pray,
If on the door I knock

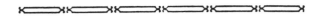

That hides so many dead,
That savagery on rock
In vain be shed.
A secret law contrives
To give time symmetry:
There is, within our lives,
An exact mystery.

From this October night
May you be given
Peace, though the trees by blight
Or storms are riven.
And though the abounding spray
Destroy what issues from it,
May time that law obey,
Strict as a comet,
Which gives in gratitude
All we give, back,
By that rich love renewed
Which misers lack.

Child, what would I not give
To change for you
The world in which we live
And make it new,
Not in the paths and towers
Of prayer and praise,
But in the outrageous powers
Their waste displays.
May night's twin mysteries,
Time's equipoise,
Call upon love, and these
Build all your joys.

1960

Serena

The cradle stirs.
There life, there innocence, there the miracle shines.
Old, he is old:
Life's earliest word, the first. Light has created him
Out of inscrutable deeps.

And the light breathes;
It breathes in darkness, trembles, trembles and wakes.
There is no help,
There is no help in this room. The divining deluge
Thunders. Time is at hand.

Who knows the print
Of feet, Christ's way, reversing the martyrs' steps,
Their counter-joy?
What fingers touch, through time stealthily flowing,
Music under the sandgrains?

What tremulous dove
Has made shoot, sink and scatter, blind and dark,
Ridges of fear,
That all must fall save him great love has lifted
To walk on his own grief?

Whose eyes now break?
Where is that head so young, it has not seen dawn?
What torches gold
Kindle the temples? What foreboding blossoms
Fall through infinite evening?

With discord, death,
Harpies and Sirens sow the furrowed sea.
Their music moves
Across the water, and the vessel whirling
Feels the destroying birds.

What holds him safe,
Lost in a chaos of conflicting waves?
What thread is wound
About him, that no Cyclops' eye may triumph
Over the singing hands?

The zenith sighs.
The voyage of Magellan breaks his sleep.
He treads the waves
Haunted by little ships whose daring reaches
Islands of spice and robbers.

He will be calm
When mutinous seas lay hold upon his ship.
When hope seems lost
And the unnameable Furies, loosed, defy him,
He will be calm at heart.

The source of time
Still binds the flying galaxies to rock.
Nothing shall change
The diamond fixed between vine-masted Noah
And the first deluge drop.

He will be calm
In the first calm that glittered before knowledge.
Nothing shall change
The *Primum Mobile's* effectual music
Planted within the breast.

He will be calm,
Not through a reason known to man, nor favour,
But through that gift
The First Cause left, printing upon his forehead
The word "Serena."

1952

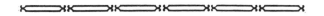

Birth and Morning

Are you come then, with the first beech leaves, stubborn
    and frail,
Dragging new brilliance out of the night of the branch
Where apple-trees move under wind, on fire from the
    wound of the grail,
Stream of wild stars for a fork-stemmed blossom to stanch?

Birth and morning: full night pulled down to the earth
Drenched by the violence of rain where the dawn wind
    dries
Buds in the trance of sunrise straining to ultimate birth,
Rigid, expecting Easter, released to the skies:

Silken they stand, weaned from the heart of light,
A splendour of water splashed from original green,
Painted with wax of creation, dazzling, hurting the sight
With a touch immaculate, fading before it has been.

I restore to the garden the footprints of one that was near
Whose arms would cradle you now, a magnanimous ghost,
But who sleeps without knowing your name in the turn
    and the quick of the year.
My eyes are fixed on the branches, my soul on the lost.

Yet here is beginning, the broken shell of a bird.
These days that will not be remembered are holy, your
    first;
The finches fly in and out while the apple-tree buds, wind-
    stirred,
Like sepulchres sleep, where no single blossom has burst.

All the morning the lawn has been filled with a
    woodpecker's cry
Awake in the shrubbery, diving from tree to tree.
The air is green with his sallies. In the wake of his
    plummage I
Divine with a leaden plummet the days to be.

I watch you here, and your eyes are closed on the cry
The woodpecker nails to the bark of the fir and the ground.
Wet from the caul of Spring are the blazing beech leaves,
    dry
The apple-trees' antlered branches where you sleep sound.

Beyond this wall the blue sea: the sap from the root
Ascends where the woodpecker clings to the fir-tree's bark.
And here, out of sight of the sea, I hear his excited shout,
The exuberant, bright-crested bird resurrecting the dark.

And you sleep under sunlight, gone with the wing to the
    dalliance
Of magical boughs, the pursuit and the pairing of birds
In the shaft of April, that perch, take fire and cavort with
    the brilliance
Of branches whose shadows interpret the lost and their
    words.

Larks sing, in the deep, dense blue, above gorse and rocks,
Black specks. Light falls where they mount. A commotion
    of wings
Rustles the furnace of thorns where blackbirds nest in the
    thicket.
The shaft the birds fly from, the shade and the phoenix, are
    Spring's.

Still child, undisturbed by their noise, none asks you to find
The water of life, the stone no philosopher found,
Or the source of that secret river which runs under time
    and the wind,
Sprung, it may be, from a chalice laid in the ground.

Few are the days gone by since you looked your first
And holy their fingers who laid it, halted in frost
Too early to wake you now to heaven in the apple-tree
    garden
Near branches knowing nothing of that which is lost.

1956

Poem for Conrad

My brothers are just out of eyeshot, conspiring against me.
  Let me crawl and surprise them.
What's for me, in this house of their gains?
My sister lies out on the lawn, a pattern of patience.
  She lies on a rug, a rug I intend to cross.
But my brothers are plotting, plotting. Their gain is my loss.
They are quick to count chocolate money, and then to eat it,
  And they quarrel over their trains.
They are never content to hold nothing, or to divide
Their spoils. They do not lie down; or not for long.
  They deal in extreme situations:
The door must be dangerous, bushes are places to hide.

  One of them dresses up in feathers
  And the other crouches,
  Endlessly running wheels over floorboards and carpet
  And chanting to make them go.

  The third comes in, in his hands a fledgling.
  He is gone again, and they are gone after him
  To watch it. Now there is nothing
  But clumsy furniture.   Is it enough,
  Enough, with extended arms, to master this floor?
  I can and will stand up.
  I, too, can walk,
  Unsteadily, but in one direction,
  Between the wall and the door,
  Towards the shouts in the garden.

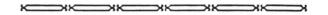

I saw nothing, but a crane has carried me in.
I am here again, and Dylan is jumping before me.
I laugh, and the louder I laugh, the higher he jumps,
First from the chair, then, in a crash, from the table,
His feet disappearing, the table's legs giving way.
I bang my cymbals, and one rolls away. He is rushing
At the wall. Chairs are behind him,
And now he is under the chairs, and he throws them up
With balls, dominoes, toys, and the tower of bricks
Falls. The crash and laughter have made me fall over.
It is wonderful here, but suddenly comes the word *No*,
And it all comes to rest, the see-saw in dancing walls,
And the feathers fallen.

I brush against dark cloth, caught up by a hand.
Snatched up to a shoulder's height,
I am told we are going to the sea.
Now, on the prickly path,
I remember something unpleasant,
The sea interfering with my enjoyment of sand.
They are talking under me, someone banging the gate
Behind us. All is blue in the air I am riding.

There are my brothers laughing and running ahead,
And a voice behind
Saying: "Whales have the sea,
And sea-lions, balancing balls, have perfect control;
But that house, those walls were not built to contain the
    exuberance
Of the performer. Let him loose
And if he continued long enough
His triumph would be complete. This would be said:
'He believed, not in walls but trumpets.
In amusing his brother he destroyed the house.' "

1961

Prime Colours

How can I praise what is not painted with
The first five colours? That winged horse of myth
Seems now a circus horse, paid to be clever:
The ride from Bethphage will last for ever.

One man may count, with imitative hooves,
The huge, high landscape that another loves,
Empound the apocalypse, till truth is pent
To satisfy the turnstiles of a tent.

Vast libraries vault their dead, but I can trust
White dust to resurrect the moving dust,
White dust of donkeys shedding dusty loads
Where swallows' wings paint Zechariah's words.

Swift, chattering swallows, flying in cloisters cool,
See through their darting eyes the imprisoned school,
Cramped, figured scribes, distorted by possession:
The upright man is always out of fashion.

Swallows come back to their first house of mud
Knowing no wider rainbow can be made;
And that first nest eclipsing heaven, that roof,
May find its image in an ass's hoof.

For when the garments and tree-branches strawed
The way a child into the mountain strayed
And on the mountain-path, in heaven's eclipse,
He found a swallow's wings, an ass's steps.

And time stopped still, stopped when an ass went down
Slowly from Bethphage to that still town.
That ass, that swallow, through the window's gap
Meet in his eyes who wears the mockers' cap.

Born of that mud, innocent light he sees,
The cornerstone in crumbling masonries.
His washed eyes, marvelling, resurrect the mountain
Where love's five colours leap into light's fountain.

1941

Music of Colours: White Blossom

White blossom, white, white shell; the Nazarene
Walking in the ear; white touched by souls
Who know the music by which white is seen,
Blinding white, from strings and aureoles,
Until that is not white, seen at the two poles,
Nor white the Scythian hills, nor Marlowe's queen.

The spray looked white until this snowfall.
Now the foam is grey, the wave is dull.
Call nothing white again, we were deceived.
The flood of Noah dies, the rainbow is lived.
Yet from the deluge of illusions an unknown colour is
    saved.

White must die black, to be born white again
From the womb of sounds, the inscrutable grain,
From the crushed, dark fibre, breaking in pain.

The bud of the apple is already forming there.
The cherry-bud, too, is firm, and behind it the pear
Conspires with the racing cloud. I shall not look.
The rainbow is diving through the wide-open book
Past the rustling paper of birch, the sorceries of bark.

Buds in April, on the waiting branch,
Starrily opening, light raindrops drench,
Swinging from world to world when starlings sweep,
Where they alight in air, are white asleep.
They will not break, not break, until you say
White is not white again, nor May May.

White flowers die soonest, die into that chaste
Bride-bed of the moon, their lives laid waste.
Lilies of Solomon, taken by the gust,
Sigh, make way. And the dark forest
Haunts the lowly crib near Solomon's dust,
Rocked to the end of majesty, warmed by the low beast,
Locked in the liberty of his tremendous rest.

If there is white, or has been white, it must have been
When His eyes looked down and made the leper clean.
White will not be, apart, though the trees try
Spirals of blossom, their green conspiracy.
She who touched His garment saw no white tree.

Lovers speak of Venus, and the white doves,
Jubilant, the white girl, myth's whiteness, Jove's,
Of Leda, the swan, whitest of his loves.
Lust imagines him, web-footed Jupiter, great down
Of thundering light; love's yearning pulls him down
On the white swan-breast, the magical lawn,
Involved in plumage, mastered by the veins of dawn.

In the churchyard the yew is neither green nor black.
I know nothing of Earth or colour until I know I lack
Original white, by which the ravishing bird looks wan.
The mound of dust is nearer, white of mute dust that dies
In the soundfall's great light, the music in the eyes,
Transfiguring whiteness into shadows gone,
Utterly secret. I know you, black swan.

                                            1942

Music of Colours: The Blossom Scattered

O, but how white is white, white from shadows come,
Sailing white of clouds, not seen before
On any snowfield, any shore;
Or this dense blue, delivered from the tomb,
White of the risen body, fiery blue of sky,
Light the saints teach us, light we learn to adore;
Not space revealed it, but the needle's eye
Love's dark thread holding, when we began to die.
It was the leper's, not the bird's cry,
Gave back that glory, made that glory more.

I cannot sound the nature of that spray
Lifted on wind, the blossoms falling away,
A death, a birth, an earthy mystery,
As though each petal stirring held the whole tree
That grew, created on the Lord's day.
There is no falling now. Yet for time's sake
These blossoms are scattered. They fall. How still they are.
They drop, they vanish, where all blossoms break.
Who touches one dead blossom touches every star.

So the green Earth is first no colour and then green.
Spirits who walk, who know
All is untouchable, and, knowing this, touch so,
Who know the music by which white is seen,
See the world's colours in flashes come and go.
The marguerite's petal is white, is wet with rain,
Is white, then loses white, and then is white again
Not from time's course, but from the living spring,
Miraculous whiteness, a petal, a wing,
Like light, like lightning, soft thunder, white as jet,
Ageing on ageless breaths. The ages are not yet.

Is there a tree, a bud, that knows not this:
White breaks from darkness, breaks from such a kiss
No mind can measure? Locked in the branching knot,
Conception shudders; that interior shade
Makes light in darkness, light where light was not;
Then the white petal, of whitest darkness made,
Breaks, and is silent. Immaculate they break,
Consuming vision, blinding eyes awake,
Dazzling the eyes with music, light's unspoken sound,
White born of bride and bridegroom, when they take
Love's path through Hades, engendered of dark ground.

Leda remembers. The rush of wings cast wide.
Sheer lightning, godhead, descending on the flood.
Night, the late, hidden waters on the moon's dark side.
Her virgin secrecy, doomed against time to run.
Morning. The visitation. All colours hurled in one.
Struggling with night, with radiance! That smothering
    glory cried:
"Heavenborn am I. White-plumaged heart, you beat against
    the sun!"
All recollection sinking from the dazzled blood.

She woke, and her awakened wings were fire,
Darkened with light; O blinding white was she
With white's bewildering darkness. So that secret choir
Know, in the thicket, and witness more than we,
Listening to early day, dew's voice, the lightest feet,
As though Saint Francis passing, told who they were,
Fledged of pure spirit, though upheld by air.
I think one living is already there
So sound asleep she is, her breath so faint,
She knows, she welcomes the footstep of the saint,
So still, so moving, joy sprung of despair,
And the two feasts, where light and darkness meet.

               1949

Music of Colours:
Dragonfoil and the Furnace of Colours

I

Bright petal, dragonfoil, springing from the hot grass,
Dazzling profusion continually fading,
Sprung from the white fire, tiger-lily, snake-fang
Basking in brilliance; deep in fume of poppies
Sleep the black stamens.

Where were these born then, nurtured of the white light?
Dragonfly, kingfisher breaking from the white bones,
Snows never seen, nor blackthorn boughs in winter,
Lit by what brand of a perpetual summer,
These and the field flowers?

All is entranced here, mazed amid the wheatfield
Mustardseed, chicory, sky of the cornflower
Deepening in sunlight, singing of the reapers,
Music of colours swaying in the light breeze,
Flame wind of poppies.

Lizards on dry stone; gipsy-bright nasturtiums
Burning through round leaves, twining out in torch-buds;
Even the stream's tongue alters where the rose-blaze
Hangs in forgetfulness. Who beneath the water
Plucks at the dark strings?

Where is the young Spring, clustered myosotis?
Have you forgotten, drugged beneath the heat haze,
White stems of bluebells hidden in the dark wood,
Swan of the lily, purple-throated iris,
Lost in your silence?

Speak: what Ophelia lies among your shadows?
Is it her music, or is it Eurydice
Gone from your bank, for there a spirit's absence
Wakens the music that was heard by Orpheus,
Lost, where the stream glides.

Far off, continually, I can hear the breakers
Falling, destroying, secret, while the rainbow,
Flying in spray, perpetuates the white light,
Ocean, kindler of us, mover and mother,
Constantly changing.

II

Brand lit in foliage, in the heart of summer,
Breaking from the live coals, torn from the seed-pod,
Flaunting its brilliance, petals of the burnet-rose
Stirred by a slow wind, under gold antennae
Wasp-gold, simmering, hovering in heat haze,
Red silk of poppies:

June wakes the music that was known to Orpheus,
Breathed by the fire-god, muted for enchantment,
Fire-misted marigold, clustered myosotis
Sprung to remember the river's lamentation,
June flowers hiding the footprints of Eurydice
Seized by the dark king.

Yet the turf tells me: she it is, no other,
Touches the rose-blaze, gathers what became her
Music. Forgetfulness holds her like a girdle
Silent. Only by absence is the song made
Audible. Orpheus, leaning above Lethe,
Knows every note there.

There the stream flies on to its own beginning,
Slips through the fresh banks, woods of their escaping,
Leaving in glory patterns of a lost world,
Leaves that are shadows of a different order,
Light, born of white light, broken by the wave's plunge
Here into colours.

Ocean, kindler of us, mover and mother,
Assailing the rock with variety of music,
Inconstancy of pattern, eternally renewing
Through mother-of-pearl the colours of destruction
Dissolving, lost in the whisper of the sea-cave,
Sigh of a gull's wings!

Here now is summer, this perennial wonder
Of fireborn blossoms, the sudden incarnation
True for this moment, therefore never dying,
Ever transfigured by the net of sunbeams,
Being of the spray, the rainbow from the breakers,
Born, like the white girl.

III

Who half asleep, or waking, does not hear it,
Drone where the bees swarm, sky of the cornflower,
Blaze of a water-lily, music of the reapers,
Lithe bodies moving continually forward
Under the heat haze?

Dust drops from campions where the hedge is hottest.
Foxgloves and grasses tremble where a snake basks,
Coiled under brilliance. Petals of the burnet-rose
Flash there, pulsating: do the gold antennae
Feel for the white light?

All that is made here hides another making;
Even this water shows a magic surface.
Sky is translated; dragonfly and iris
Rise from the grey sheath; unremembered shadows
Cling, where the bloom breaks.

Yet, not that bloom, nor any kind of foliage,
Cup, sheath or daystar, bright above the water,
Clustered forget-me-nots tufted on the stream's bank,
Not one recalls the virginals of April
Heard, when the wood grieved.

Waking entranced, we cannot see that other
Order of colours moving in the white light.
Time is for us transfigured into colours
Known and remembered from an earlier summer,
Or into breakers.

Falling on gold sand, bringing all to nothing.
Fire of the struck brand hides beneath the white spray.
All life begins there, scattered by the rainbow;
Yes, and the field flowers, these deceptive blossoms,
Break from the furnace.

1960

Music of Colours: The Cave
(fragment)

Enter, naked. Rock, washed by the sea,
Brilliant above the embroidered foam, sings:
"Waves break, unrobing so many dead.
Why do you come here, why, whom to set free
After a thousand ages? Only rings
Speak of those fingers, stones of the unadorned head."

No. I come to tell you: "You are yourself,
Flushed by mysterious colours, about to be born.
Why do you flash in bewilderment, green and red?
Frail as the delicate seabird's egg on the shelf,
Hard as the spiral shell's enclosing horn,
I know a gift for those hands, for the unadorned head."

What is that gift? Rock, washed by the sea

(unpublished)

Evening
(fragment)

Evening, father of us, preternatural starlight,
Beginning of wonder, fingers of darkness,
Hold us, heal us, and send us praising
Out on our journey.

1969

The Lady with the Unicorn

About this lady many fruitful trees.
There the chaste unicorn before her knees
Stares in a glass to purify her sight.
At her right hand a lion sits,
And through the foliage, in and out, there flits
Many a bird; then hounds, with deer in flight:
Light is her element; her tapestry is light.

There is her mediaeval music met.
On the high table-top, with damask set
To charm, between the chaste beast and the strong,
An organ which her fingers play
Rests, and her pretty servant's hands obey
Those pipes with bellows to sustain their song
Attuned to distant stars, making their short life long.

This ended, gathered from some leafy way,
That servant brings her flowers upon a tray.
She lifts them to inhale their magic breath.
Caught in that breath's elusive maze,
She marvels. On a stool a monkey plays
With flowers from wicker trailing, strewn beneath,
A heaven of fragrance breathing through their mask of
    death.

Next, her right hand upholds the coat-of-arms
Seeming love's guardian against war's alarms,
And with her left she grips the upright horn.
This touch, while birds through branches peer,
Consecrates all the beasts as they appear,
Frisking among dark foliage to adorn
Her fingers that caress the constant unicorn.

A lion rampant grips the upright pole.
Her serving-maid now proffers her a bowl
Of peaches, damsons, almonds, grapes, and sweets.
This lady savours one, and sees
How white of almonds, red of mulberries,
Is each a praise no other tree repeats,
Now strangely on love's tree engrafted while she eats.

The senses leave a chain upon her tongue.
That place is hushed, from which the light is sprung.
Curtains are hung, embroidered with strange art.
The letters "TO MY SOLE DESIRE"
Crown that pavilion with a band of fire
Whose folds the unicorn and lion part,
Revealing in their midst her love-awakened heart.

O sovereign balm to heal all mortal illness:
Long let him look, and still he will find stillness,
Her one betrothed, who sees her museful face.
This lady, with her flowers and hounds,
Woven in light, in air, in wooded grounds,
Transmits a glory wrought about her grace,
Caught in a sacred bond within the encircling space.

Let him look softly, with some seventh sense
Breaking that circle's hushed magnificence,
And see what universe her love controls,
Moving with hushed, divine intent
Through the five senses to their sacrament
Whose Eden turns between two silent poles,
Creating with pure speed that harmony of souls.

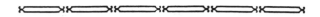

Where is the heart of mathematic space?
Throned on a mystery in that leafy place,
This lady's fingers hold, where distance flies,
The Past and Future like a skein
For her betrothed to wind, and loose again.
Lion and unicorn forbid disguise.
He looks, and she looks forth: there are no other eyes.

1948

The Turning of the Leaves

Not yet! Do not yet touch,
Break not this branch of silver-birch,
Nor ask the stealthy river why it laves
Black roots that feed the leaves.

Ask first the flickering wren.
He will move further. Ask the rain.
No drop, though round, through that white miracle
Will sink, to be your oracle.

Not yet! Do not yet bend
Close to that root so tightly bound
Loosened by creeping waters as they run
Along the fork's rough groin.

Ask not the water yet
Why the root's tapering tendrils eat
Parched earth away that they may be
Nearer the source those fibres must obey.

Behind the bark your hands will find
No Sycorax or flying Daphne faned
And the brown ignorant water bindweed breeds
Not caring there what brows it braids.

Light in the branches weaves.
Hard is the waiting moment while it waves,
This tree whose trunk curves upward from the stream
Where faltering ripples strum.

See how it hangs in air.
The leaves are turning now. We cannot hear
The death and birth of life. But that disguise,
Look up now, softly: break it with your eyes.

1937

The Turning of the Stars

There is a moment when Apollo's tree
Is Daphne still. The Past is not the Past
But wound within a ring
So finely wrought,
It knows each path and avenue of thought.
Downward he looks, through heaven and earth, to see
The sunlight and dayspring
Caught in her eyes, all uttered love surpassed
By that first heaven which knows her timelessly.

There is a touch, before the wall of bark
Echoes the music of those timeless hands,
The pivot of the god
Like light revealed
Where all the stars seem fallen in one field,
And secret, where the underleaf is dark,
Language is understood
Green as a spring, translated for all lands,
A touch to which rivers of leaves must hark.

Look. In the midnight heaven two stars draw near,
First the awakening laurel pressed by lips,
Her mortal destiny,
Her walk, her grief,
Then her ascending star of true belief;
Opposed, of differing glories, they appear,
Each on its axle-tree
Whirling, two heavenly bodies, to eclipse,
Pitched into darkness by love's greater year.

Miraculous, the flight of measured thought
Crosses the rebel fire of burning youth;
A choir of tranquil heads
Moving sublime
Through Raphael's heaven, from distance into time,
Inspired the pupil Perugino taught
To paint heaven's periods,
His mind being in its silence fixed on truth:
Unrest in calm, calm in unrest he sought.

Galileo, spun, recanting, to the stars,
Through the smoked glass of time presumed to watch
With monstrous emphasis
The disc of light
Edged by the rim of that great wheel in flight;
Copernicus proclaimed, we turned like Mars;
He checked the sun by this.
Alighieri, fixed yet flying, knelt to match
The speed of distance to the burial-vase.

Circle on circle, purgatorial years
Whirl against time the union of the blest.
A man may bind the stars
To his own bent
By faith protected, till that grave ascent
Find a new pivot for the moving spheres;
Or this may come to pass:
One intense moment may consume the rest,
A flash translate blind mortals into seers.

So love descends: the star which blots out heaven
Moves in the morning of our making hands.
Where Raphael's heavens project
On Mary's dread
The Infant Christ, a halo round His head,
He seems, the firstfruits of their sleep, to have given
To living intellect
The life of faith their death in faith demands;
His broken bread affirmed the sleepers' leaven.

About us garlands of earth's natural green
Quicken with May and hide the blackbird's clutch.
Leaves cover up the well,
And buds begin
To break, and hide the fountain's origin.
Spring behind Spring, star behind star, unseen,
Revolve in seed and cell.
Vision fulfils the source of visible touch.
Invisible dancers make our feet serene.

There is a power that holds me by a chain,
So ancient is the love that guards this book,
Inscrutable that praise;
I see the crash,
Fleece and spent fury, Sodom's deluge-flash;
I see the wide world sink, and rise again,
Hung in pure night, ablaze
With million worlds united in a look
Where boundless glory astounds the eye of the brain.

Verse is a part of silence. I have known
Always that declamation is impure.
This language best fits prayer,
The crystal night
Teeming with worlds in mathematic height.
Prodigious darkness guards its undertone,
And though that wheel of air
Seems to leave nothing earthly to endure,
The likeness, not the original, is gone.

1948

Testimony

She testifies to that first truth
The hour-glass cannot hold.
Her voice recalls the voice of Ruth
When she to Naomi told
A pledge too dear for time to break
Or Earth to render vain:
Dark is the radiance doomed to wake
This Danae to the rain.

Delicate as the foal whose hooves
Seem moving on the sky,
Clear as the questioning moon that moves
And feels the waves' reply,
Fragrant as when Spring rains renew
The lilac and the lime,
Rich as the Earth which Adam knew
Before the birth of time:

In every form I see the stamp
And image of the fair,
And yet Copernicus's lamp
Was always burning there.
How could interpreters divine
The depth of eye and hand
If the lost myth that made them shine
They could not understand?

Put out that lamp, and let her be
Cut from the sacred cord,
From bright Eternity set free,
Weaned by a pagan word;
A life courageous, short and great
As in the days gone by,
Spun by the strong, blind-fingered Fate,
Restore, and let her die.

No use! The measure of her days
Sinks, to outlive the moon,
Shines like the widow's cruse of praise
And is restored as soon,
That watched Elijah on the bed
Bowed in the might of prayer
Bring back the breath into his dead
And give her son to her.

What's faith? Her movement in repose
Hangs by so fine a thread.
The fountain fills and overflows:
What patience there is shed,
Making her plunge of glory seem
A prey to hungry time,
Whose planets through the elliptic beam
Back to their stations climb.

1950

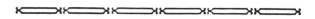

Foal

Darkness is not dark, nor sunlight the light of the sun
But a double journey of insistent silver hooves.
Light wakes in the foal's blind eyes as lightning illuminates
    corn
With a rustle of fine-eared grass, where a starling shivers.

And whoever watches a foal sees two images,
Delicate, circling, born, the spirit with blind eyes leaping
And the left spirit, vanished, yet here, the vessel of ages
Clay-cold, blue, laid low by her great wide belly the hill.

See him break that circle, stooping to drink, to suck
His mother, vaulted with a beautiful hero's back
Arched under the singing mane,
Shaped to her shining, pricked into awareness
By the swinging dug, amazed by the movement of suns;
His blue fellow has run again down into grass,
And he slips from that mother to the boundless horizons of
    air,
Looking for that other, the foal no longer there.

But perhaps
In the darkness under the tufted thyme and downtrodden
    winds,
In the darkness under the violet's roots, in the darkness of
    the pitcher's music,
In the uttermost darkness of a vase
There is still the print of fingers, the shadow of waters.
And under the dry, curled parchment of the soil there is
    always a little foal
Asleep.

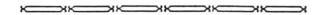

So the whole morning he runs here, fulfilling the track
Of so many suns; vanishing the mole's way, moving
Into mole's mysteries under the zodiac,
Racing, stopping in the circle. Startled he stands
Dazzled, where darkness is green, where the sunlight is
    black,
While his mother, grazing, is moving away
From the lagging star of those stars, the unrisen wonder
In the path of the dead, fallen from the sun in her hooves,
And eluding the dead hands, begging him to play.

                                    1941

The Mare

The mare lies down in the grass where the nest of the
    skylark is hidden.
Her eyes drink the delicate horizon moving behind the
    song.
Deep sink the skies, a well of voices. Her sleep is the vessel
    of Summer.
That climbing music requires the hidden music at rest.

Her body is utterly given to the light, surrendered in
    perfect abandon
To the heaven above her shadow, still as her first-born day.
Softly the wind runs over her. Circling the meadow, her
    hooves
Rest in a race of daisies, halted where butterflies stand.

Do not pass her too close. It is easy to break the circle
And lose that indolent fullness rounded under the ray
Falling on light-eared grasses your footstep must not yet
    wake.
It is easy to darken the sun of her unborn foal at play.

1952

The Replica

Once more the perfect pattern falls asleep,
And in the dark of sleep the replica
Springs to awareness. Light is born of dark
As the young foal beside his mother steps,
Closer than her own shadow. All runs down
To agile youth, born of laborious age.
She feels his presence in the pulse of earth,
Entranced above her pasture, how his eyes
From that new darkness at the end of time
In wonder stare, astonished by her world.
Each pristine, airy venture is prescribed
By weight of the maternal shade he left,
The circle ending where his race began.

The waterfall by falling is renewed
And still is falling. All its countless changes
Accumulate to nothing but itself.
The voice of many mountains or of one,
The dissipation of unnumbered drops
Vanishing in a dark that finds itself
In a perpetual music, and gives light
In fading always from the measuring mind:
Such is the waterfall; and though we watch it
Falling from rock to rock and always changing,
Cast to a whirlpool, pent by rock, pursuing
A reckless path, headlong in radiant mist
Leaping within the roar of its own chains,
We know it lives by being consumed, we know
Its voice is new and ancient, and its force
Flies from single impulse that believes
Nothing is vain, though all is cast for sorrow.
There hangs the image of our life, there flies

The image of our transience. If you ask
Where may divinity or love find rest
When all moves forward to a new beginning
And each obeys one constant law of change,
I cannot answer.
                Yet to man alone,
Moving in time, birth gives a timeless movement,
To taste the secret of the honeycomb
And pluck from night that blessing which outweighs
All the calamities and griefs of time.
There shines the one scene worthy of his tears,
For in that dark the greatest light was born
Which, if man sees, then time is overthrown,
And afterwards all acts are qualified
By knowledge of that interval of glory:
Music from heaven, the incomparable gift
Of God to man, in every infant's eyes
That vision which is ichor to the soul
Transmitted there by lightning majesty,
The replica, reborn, of Christian love.

                                      1959

Sycamore

O, I am green and fair:
Is there a fairer tree?
Who is it underneath
Sleeps the sleep of death?
There is no answer there.
There is no answer there.

Centuries made me firm.
Far I have spread my roots.
I grip the flying stream.
Aching, I drop my fruits.
Who is it sleeps below?
Who is it sleeps below?

My wood made long ago
Lutes of true, hollow sound.
Lovers still carve them out
Above this burial mound.
Who is it sleeps below?
Who is it sleeps below?

Who sleeps? The young streams feed
My boughs. The blind keys spin.
Hark, he is dead indeed.
Never shall fall again
My natural, winged seed
On this small-statured man.

1941

Zacchaeus in the Leaves

Silence before
Sound.
Sycamore:

A tree
Predestined to beauty.
Blown leaves. Antiquity.
Light lost. Light found.

The myth above the myth.
The imagined zenith
Of youth in youth.

Light on the leaves in wind
Flying. The silver-sequined
Goat-leaf, dark-skinned.

Sycamore leaves; coiled thick,
God-dark, Dionysiac,
The ascending trunk. Pan's music.
The sap made quick.

Wind-gathered sound. The flow
Of lives. Wood-sounds. Wood-hollow.
Hades locked below.

Sap leaps. The springing race
Threading the magic surface
Drops to one place.

A sign to us!
A tree, and then a tree
No more.

Silent Zacchaeus,
Ageless one.
The buried sun,
And the key it bore.

*   *   *

Light found in every age
The leaves of Spring
Fading from lineage,
The seed, the wing.

From what dark scent
Of waters breaking
In night most innocent
Of dead men waking,

From what laid bone
Rose man's belief?
What Sibyl wrote upon
The breaking leaf?

Sibylline words.
The buried lives.
Lost among nesting-birds,
The burden of the leaves.

The myth above the myth,
Pan above Zacchaeus;
Zacchaeus climbing,
Mounted above his youth,
Alone in time
Seeking the heavenly death.

The crooked he had left,
Yes, and the wise,
To climb the tree-trunk,
To sit in a cleft
And see through his eyes
Not what they saw,
Not what they heard,
No leaf, no claw,
No wing, no bird,
But light surpassing
All known green,
As if all drunk
And sober stirred,
Known, unknown,
Where seen, unseen,
Were one alone;
Jesus passing,
The Nazarene.

Lovers embraced
And their eyes were solaced;
But Zacchaeus gripped fast

The tree-branch, crouching,
Watching the myth
Moving, the myth
Move to the zenith
Not found in youth:
"If His eyes see us,
If His eyes see us,
Dazzled above men,
Though we are buried then,
The myth above the truth."

Who stilled the pipes of Pan?
What marvel weaves
Death, deathless, pagan,
Turning the Sibyl's leaves?

Firm, yet betrayed no more,
The young lie with the young.
Leaves of the sycamore,
Lifted on wind, give tongue:

"I have supported one
In my own right
Who watched the procession,
His eyes full of light.

I can fade now,
My thought heard or unheard.
Did he not leave my bough,
And said no word?"

*　　*　　*

Slow the procession was coming. The drinkers remained
Sitting cross-legged, close to the dead who were chained,
Beggars of light. Only the man in the tree
Looked on the road, and saw where light was ordained.

Among the quick and the dead is the point divine,
Moving; among those talking, the drinkers of wine,
The shuffling of feet, the running of time, the gust
Of windblown leaves, no, not the Muses, the nine,

Have seen the universe race through the leaves and thrill
Because it has found the point of predestined will,
There where the fountain breaks from lips that are dust.
Stop: the great branches are moving. Now they are still.

1945

Loiterers

This my birthplace? No, friend, this is Xanion's,
He, the owner of that yellow barley.
Mischievous chicory was all I planted:
Blue-eyed, we played here.

O, could the mayfly of memory wing back
Through bee-bustle and waspish digressions,
Certainly here it would find us standing,
Left in this cart-rut.

There the house glinted, near the tilting hay-rick,
Down through rose-ramblers to the prosperous earth-
    mould.
There the sky flashed to the windows, and the windows
Flashed to our young eyes.

Dawn's early singers, missel-thrush and skylark,
Still mark the track we followed to the cornfield.
Foxgloves in midge-light hid the turning river
Swept by the swallows.

Fallen is the house to the earth-mould, fallen.
Quick, for we lag here. If the dust is pollen
Robbed by the butterfly, stolen by the mayfly,
Why should we sigh, then?

1952

A Man with a Field

If I close my eyes I can see a man with a load of hay
Cross this garden, guiding his wheelbarrow through the
    copse
To a long, low green-house littered with earthenware, glass
    and clay,
Then prop his scythe near the sycamore to enter it, potted
    with seeds,
And pause where chrysanthemums grow, with tomatoes'
    dragonish beads.
Stooping to fasten the door, he turns on the path which
    leads
To his rain-pitted bedroom of cellos, and low jugs catching
    the drops.

If I open my eyes I see this musician-turned-ploughman
    slow,
Plainly follow his tractor vibrating beneath blue sky,
Or cast his sickle wide, or reach full-length with the hoe,
Or blame the weather that set its blight on a crop or a plan
To mend his roof, or cut back trees where convolvulus ran,
Or attend to as many needs as the holes in a watering-can:
He would wait for the better weather; it had been a wet
    July.

This year his field lay fallow; he was late putting down his
    seed.
Cold December concealed with a sighing surplice of snow
His waste of neglected furrows, overgrown with mutinous
    weed.

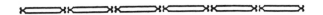

Dark, bereaved like the ground, I found him feeble and sick,
And cold, for neither the sticks nor his lamp with a
    shrunken wick
Would light. He was gone through the wicket. His clock
    continued to tick,
But it stopped when the new flakes clustered on an empty
    room below.

1951

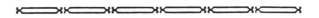

The Scythe

Custom shall not restore
The scythe to its old place,
Not with the selfsame hand,
Nor leave a single trace
Outside the greenhouse door
Of him who owned this land.

Yet when I look I see
A stooping figure pass
With his low-handled barrow
Trundling a load of grass
Where now the abounding tree
Has lost his flashing shadow.

Within that gloom the bough
Inclines Zacchaeus' keys
Not ready yet to fall.
Lift the scythe's edge to please
His testing hand who now
Remains beyond recall,

Leaning above his blade
Near the long-shadowed sheaves,
Guarded by that true stone
Under the Summer leaves
On which an edge is made
When the last light is gone.

1953

Kestrel

Kestrel, king of small hawks, moreover
Keenest of sight, blind wings you shake,
Pinned on the sky, and, quivering, hover

High over prey. A gloom you make
Hang from one point in changing time
On grass. Below you seawaves break

Rebellious, casting rhyme on rhyme
Vainly against the craggy world
From whose black death the ravens climb.

Stand then in storm; see fragments whirled
And pitched by waters to a place
Where wave on wave in mockery hurled

Shake the great sea-rock to its base.
And still the inviolate wing and claw
Hold chaos in the grip of grace.

High on the rock's grass verge you saw
Your quarry. You above that rock
Hung by inscrutable, patient law,

Motionless. Then you plunged, a block
Between that headland and the sky
Hiding you. Stalling in their flock

The startled herring-gulls gave cry,
Sprung from a sea of beaten flame.
Bird of my wrist, inspired you fly.

Who dares to think the storm untame
Can hurt or master you whom I,
Gathering the doom of all who die,
Uplift, in every age, the same?

1954

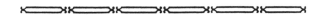

Ophelia

Stunned in the stone light, laid among the lilies,
Still in the green wave, graven in the reed-bed,
Lip-read by clouds in the language of the shallows,
Lie there, reflected.

Soft come the eddies, cold between your fingers.
Rippling through cresses, willow-trunk and reed-root,
Gropes the grey water; there the resting mayfly
Burns like an emerald.

Haunting the path, Laertes falls to Hamlet;
He, the young Dane, the mover of your mountains,
Sees the locked lids, your nunnery of sorrows,
Drowned in oblivion.

Silvered with dawn, the pattern of the bridge-vault
Dancing, a light-skein woven by the stream there,
Travels through shade the story of your dying,
Sweet-named Ophelia.

Dense was your last night, thick with stars unnumbered.
Bruised, the reeds parted. Under them the mud slipped,
Yielding. Scuttling and terrified, the moorhen
Left you to sink there.

Few, faint the petals carried on the surface,
Watched by those bright eyes ambushed under shadow,
Mouse, bird and insect, bore you witness, keeping
Pace ever silent.

Here, then, you lingered, late upon the world's rim,
Matched here the princelike, stopped, and were
    confounded,
Finding that image altered in the water's
Bitter remembrance.

Passion recalls the tumult of your story,
Midnight revives it, where your name is printed;
Yet from the water, intimate, there echoes:
"Tell this to no man."

Bride-veils of mist fall, brilliant are the sunbeams,
Open the great leaves, all the birds are singing.
Still unawake in purity of darkness
Whiter than daylight

Dream the soft lids, the white, the deathly sleeping;
Closed are the lashes: day is there a legend.
Rise from the fair flesh, from the midnight water,
Child too soon buried.

1946

Ruth's Lament for Naomi

I cannot count the times we met.
You clasped me near the field of hay.
I stood when Orpah would not stay.
Now death has brought us closer yet.

O mother, whom no lips have sung,
A seal is laid upon my tongue.
I watch the waters glide away
And guard the image they forget.

1950

The Yew-tree

Is there a cause why we should wake the dead?
Should they not sleep, safe in the sepulchre?
I, a man walking, one alive to fear,
Hear these deep, holy boughs and berries red
Sweep the dark graves, then stop where seem to tread
Long-vanished mourners from an earlier year.
Late-leaving, then, from each fresh grave I hear
Love's nearmost: "O, who will lift this lost, loved head,
Crowned with flowers fading, whose quick colours pray?"
Then none makes answer; yet, soon, bodily
Reaching to God, I hear that good thief say:
"Lord, for no wrong Thou diest, but justly we."
That word kills grief, and through the dark-boughed tree
Gives to each dead his resurrection day.

1947

Green Names, Green Moss

The grief-rung, searching bell
Vaulted with footprints flying
Proclaims the pangs of hell
Altered by the dying.
They are gone in. I wait
By the grave's single flower
Where mosses ruminate
On birthday and death-hour.
What earthquake undermines
The general burial-ground,
Altering the proud lines
To a parable unfound?
The mourners all were wrong
Who followed them from towns,
Under the tempters' song
Of eunuch bells and gowns
To these twin tenements,
Obscurity and Fame,
Cold seed of great events
And sleep's last epigram.

Swing, life-leaping bell;
Strike, in the mourning trees.
No ravisher can tell
Their secret histories;
Not one can you reclaim,
But side-track their loss
Until the last, loved name
Is covered with moss.
Yet every moment must,
Each turn of head or hand,
Though disfigured by dust,

Incorruptibly stand;
If they are nothing now
Then they were nothing then.
Blinded with thirst I know,
Beneath my foot lie men
Each laid in his own caul
Too intricately still
In the rock of his soul
Where the pure fountains fill,
Too sacred to be touched
By memory or bell.
Out of wild hands that clutched,
Their lives, vibrating, fell.
The echoes breed children
Where the round bell swings.
A crippled coupling tune
Old Charon sings
As with an ivied oar
He rows across.
I can see them no more,
Only green names, green moss.

1944

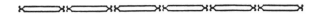

Gravestones

Look down. The dead have life.
Their dreadful night accompanies our Springs.
Touch the next leaf:
Such darkness lives there, where a last grief sings.

Light blinds the whirling graves.
Lost under rainwet earth the letters run.
A finger grieves,
Touching worn names, bearing daughter and son.

Here the quick life was borne,
A fountain quenched, fountains with sufferings crowned.
Creeds of the bone
Summoned from darkness what no Sibyl found.

Truly the meek are blest
Past proud men's trumpets, for they stilled their fame
Till this late blast
Gave them their muted, and their truest name.

Sunk are the stones, green-dewed,
Blunted with age, touched by cool, listening grass.
Vainly these died,
Did not miraculous silence come to pass.

Yet they have lovers' ends,
Lose to hold fast, as violets root in frost.
With stronger hands
I see them rise through all that they have lost.

I take a sunflower down,
With light's first faith persuaded and entwined.
Break, buried dawn,
For the dead live, and I am of their kind.

1945

For a Wine Festival

Now the late fruits are in.
Now moves the leaf-starred year
Down, in the sun's decline,
Stoop. Have no fear.
Glance at the burdened tree:
Dark is the grape's wild skin.
Dance, limbs, be free.
Bring the bright clusters here
And crush them into wine.

Acorns from yellow boughs
Drop to the listening ground.
Spirits who never tire,
Dance, dance your round.
Old roots, old thoughts and dry,
Catch as your footprints rouse
Flames where they fly,
Knowing the year has found
Its own more secret fire.

Nothing supreme shall pass.
Earth to an ember gone
Wears but the death it feigns
And still burns on.
One note more true than time
And shattered falls his glass.
Steal, steal from rhyme:
Take from the glass that shone
The vintage that remains.

1966

Returning from Harvest

It is always so: the declining
Daylight touching the edge
Of a window quickens knowledge,
Whets the invisible wing

Of thought, as the mist-hazed hummer
Michaelmas patterns weaves.
The stream understands the leaves
Better than in high summer.

And however the intellect
Predict the pattern of days,
It is never repeated. Always
A change we did not expect

Interprets the sickle gleaning
High sheaves for a sheltered place.
A young moon hangs in space
But shines with a different meaning.

Evening never deceives
Man, as the waggon swings
Back from migrating wings
To his mud-encrusted eaves.

They are gone before the stoat
In the iron track dawn-fires smelt
Changes his chestnut pelt
For the white of the ermine's coat.

O freshness of the precise
Season, frost-clear sky,
Full harvest tilted high
In the ruts of tomorrow's ice.

1961

Fidelities

The fountain gathers, in a single jet,
Fidelities where beams together run,
Thrives upon loss, enriches us with debt.

Nothing will match the day's full unison.
I love to see light break; and yet, and yet,
The final arbiter is not the sun.

Bounteous that brother, but he will forget
Others whose eyes the hand of death has closed,
Nor touch, nor seek them, when their light has set.

Seeing of what compound splendour life's composed,
Who could believe it now a part once played,
With so much owing to so many a ghost?

Of love's stern language noblest lives are made.
The shell of speech by many a voice is shot
Whose light, once kindled, cannot be betrayed.

A certain cadence underlies the plot;
However fatally the thread is spun,
The dying man can rise above his lot.

For me neglect and world-wide fame were one.
I was concerned with those the world forgot,
In the tale's ending saw its life begun;

And I was with them still when time was not.

1962

NOTES

Key to abbreviations used for reference to the volume of poems by Vernon Watkins in which each poem appears:

ML   Ballad of the Mari Lwyd (Faber, 1941)
LU   The Lady with the Unicorn (Faber, 1948)
DB   The Death Bell (Faber, 1954)
CA   Cypress and Acacia (Faber, 1959)
A   Affinities (Faber, 1962)
F   Fidelities (Faber, 1968)
UP   Uncollected Poems (Enitharmon Press, 1969)

Unity of the Stream: from F.
Poets, in Whom Truth Lives: from CA.
Touch with your Fingers: from CA.
Swallows over the Weser: from LU.
Crowds: from LU.
Fidelity to the Dead: from LU.
Fidelity to the Living: from LU.
   The poem "Mother and Child" in ML is on the same theme: both poems were inspired by Caitlin Thomas and her son Llewelyn.
Ballad of the Trial of Sodom: from DB.
   For the origin of this poem see Genesis XVIII, 23-33.
Ballad of Culver's Hole: from DB.
   In a note prepared as an introduction for public readings of this poem, Vernon Watkins wrote:
   The Ballad of Culver's Hole is about the deceptions of the sea. It is about a smuggler's cave on the Gower Coast where I live. The cave is partly the work of nature and partly the work of man. Its vertical walls rise from a bed of sand and shingle like a town with a number of look-out windows. The sea reaches its base very quickly so that the cave is not accessible at high tide. Thousands of bricks are cemented into the walls, and there are also niches of stone built into the interior at frequent intervals, rising in a spiral to the top, which is open to the sky. It is thought that hundreds of years ago these were used for keeping doves. The word Culver means a dove. But tradition has made the cave notorious for smuggling, and as a child I heard much about the smuggler whom I call Culver in the poem.

    The deception and mystery belonging to the cave extend to its surroundings. So strange is the rock formation there that the cave acquires a natural camouflage as the tide comes in. It is very difficult to see it from an angle, huge though it is when you come to it face to face. And the deeper the tide, the more suddenly the sea comes in, with a deceptive and unnatural speed.

Ballad of Hunt's Bay: from *DB.*

In an introductory note for readings of this poem Vernon Watkins wrote:

    Hunt's Bay is about a mile from my home. It is one of the rockiest bays on the coast, a crescent, or, at low tide, a dark half-moon of rocks, bounded on either side by steep cliffs and jutting boulders of whitish rock. I have seen this bay littered with wreckage from which one could build half a ship. The ballad is about a man moving among such wreckage. While he is groping among the wood he feels a presence at his side which he cannot quite see when he turns round. He has the image of a man riding a horse, but when he turns, this merges with the white horses of the waves. Then the presence speaks to him through his inner ear, and he becomes mesmerised by the wood. He sees the sunk ship floating while he touches its wreckage, and Future and Past become confused. So they must merge in the closed eyes of the drowned, and the illumination of this ballad comes from the wood itself.

Rhossili: from *LU.*

This poem refers to the headland of Rhossili which ends the Gower Peninsula. Rhossili Sands are the scene of Dylan Thomas's story "Extraordinary Little Cough" in his *Portrait of the Artist as a Young Dog.*

Taliesin in Gower: from *DB.*

This and the next five poems, which have not been printed together before, all refer to the legend of Taliesin. For the poet's source *see* the Mabinogi of Taliesin in Lady Charlotte Guest's translation of *The Mabinogion.* Pwlldu, Oxwich and Three Cliffs are all bays on the south coast of the Gower Peninsula. In verse 10 the poet refers to remains of prehistoric animals discovered during an archaeological survey begun in 1943 by E. E. Allen and J. G. Rutter. Their survey results were published in Swansea by Vaughan Thomas, in a pamphlet entitled *Gower Caves.*

Taliesin and the Spring of Vision: from *CA.*

Taliesin's Voyage: from *A.*

Verse 6 refers to the local tradition that the child Taliesin's coracle was beached at Pwlldu.

Taliesin and the Mockers: from *A.*

Verse 29 was added after the poem's first publication in 1955.

Taliesin at Pwlldu: from *F.*

Sea Chant: from *F.*

In this poem, the poet breaks away from the traditional Taliesin legends and uses the Taliesin *persona* to represent the conflict between the poet in poetry and the poet in love—a recurring theme in the poetry of Vernon Watkins: see "Stone Footing" (*ML*); "Ballad of the Three Coins" (*DB*); "Ballad of Crawley Woods" (*DB*); and, in a different context, "The Peacocks" (*LU*) and "The Crane" (*A*).

The Tributary Seasons: from *CA.*

According to the legend, St. Hubert was hunting in the forest as a young man on Good Friday when he came upon a stag bearing the crucifix between its antlers. This event converted the young man to Christianity, and the stag with the crucifix became the emblem of the saint.

Returning to Goleufryn: from *LU.*

Goleufryn was in Picton Place, Carmarthen. In verse 4, line 9, the horse's iron-shod hoof strikes sparks from the flints of the cobbled road.

Llewelyn's Chariot: from *LU.*

This poem was written for the poet's godson, Llewelyn Thomas, son of Dylan and Caitlin Thomas. Verse 3, line 6 refers to the Thomases' house at Laugharne, "Sea View."

The Caryatids: from *DB.*

This poem and the four which follow were for the poet's five children.

The Precision of the Wheel: from *A.*

The reference in verse 2 is to the collection *The Lady with the Unicorn,* which the poet was preparing on the night when his son was born.

Serena: from *CA.*

Birth and Mourning: from *CA.*

Dylan Thomas died in November 1953; the poet's son Dylan was

born in April 1954; Dylan Thomas was to have been his godfather.

Poems for Conrad: from *F.*

Prime Colours: from *ML.*

This poem introduces the five "music of colours" poems which follow, and are now printed together for the first time. In these poems, the colours of pagan myth are transfigured in the light of Christian revelation. The last two poems, of which "Music of Colours: The Cave" is here printed for the first time, are incomplete fragments; Vernon Watkins had not finished working out this theme when he died in 1967.

Music of Colours: White Blossom: from *LU.*

Music of Colours: The Blossom Scattered: from *DB.*

Music of Colours: Dragonfoil and the Furnace of Colours: from *A.*

Music of Colours: The Cave: from an unpublished manuscript.

Evening (fragment): from *UP.*

The Lady with the Unicorn: from *LU.*

The poem is concerned with the *Dame à la Licorne* tapestries in the Musée de Cluny in Paris. There are six tapestries: one on each of the five senses, and one which celebrates the betrothal of the lovers. The Unicorn, symbol of chastity and of Christ, appears in every one.

The Turning of the Leaves: from *ML.*

This and the next poem are concerned with what is permanent and what is transient. The Christian sees what is transient to pagan belief as having permanence.

The Turning of the Stars: from *DB.*

Testimony: from *DB.*

Foal: from *LU.*

This and the next two poems are held by some critics to deal with the Platonic theory of forms.

The Mare: from *CA.*

The Replica: from *CA.*

Sycamore: from *ML.*

The story of Zacchaeus referred to in this and the next poem is in Luke XIX, 1-10. Both poems deal with the recurrent theme of the conflict between pagan myths and Christian stories; *see also* "The Song of the Good Samaritan" (*LU*), where the subject is treated more fully.

Zacchaeus in the Leaves: from *LU.*

Loiterers: from *CA.*
This unusual poem was written for a *New Statesman* competition, in which it won a prize. The first line was given to competitors as a starting-point.
A Man with a Field: from *CA.*
This and the following poem are about the old man who built The Garth, Pennard Cliffs, where the poet lived. He was a man of many talents, and played the cello at The Grand Theatre, Swansea.
The Scythe: from *CA.*
Kestrel: from *CA.*
This poem deals with the recurring theme of the poet as hawk.
Ophelia: from *LU.*
Ruth's Lament for Naomi: from *CA.*
The story is from Ruth I, 14-18.
The Yew-tree: from *LU.*
The Good Thief may be found in Luke XXIII, 39-43.
Green Names, Green Moss: from *LU.*
Gravestones: from *LU.*
For a Wine Festival: from *F.*
Returning from Harvest: from *A.*
Fidelities: from *F.*

BLACK SWAN BOOKS

Catalogue available